radar

being a
stuntman

Isabel Thomas

Published in 2013 by Wayland

Copyright © Wayland 2013

Wayland
Hachette Children's Books
338 Euston Road
London NW1 3BH

Wayland Australia
Level 17/207 Kent Street
Sydney NSW 2000

Concept by Joyce Bentley

Commissioned by Debbie Foy and
Rasha Elsaeed

Produced for Wayland by Calcium
Designer: Paul Myerscough
Editor: Sarah Eason

British Library Cataloguing in Publication Data

Being a stuntman. — (Top jobs)(Radar)
   1. Stunt performers—Juvenile literature.
   I. Series
   791.4'3'028'092-dc23

ISBN: 978 0 7502 7847 8

Printed in China

  0 9 8 7 6 5 4 3 2 1

Wayland is a division of Hachette Children's Books,
an Hachette UK company.

www.hachette.co.uk

Acknowledgements: Alamy: AF archive 29, Interfoto
28–29; Corbis: David Appleby/Buena Vista Pictures/
Bureau L.A. Collection 8; Paul Darnell: 2b, 18–19;
Dreamstime: Ben Heys 3l, 23b, Linqong 23c, Marion
Wear 21; Flickr: B Furlong 25, Rob Young 16-17;
iStock: Greg Epperson 24b, Jurie Maree cover;
Rex: Mike Forster/Daily Mail 10–11; Luci Romberg: 2t,
6–7, 7bc; Shutterstock: Eniko Balogh 4–5, 12, 26–27,
Helga Esteb 13, Germanskydiver 7br, Mayskyphoto
30–31, Christophe Michot 2–3, Gabi Moisa 1,
PJ Morley 7bl, Jordan Tan 3br, 23t; Mark Wagner:
2c, 14; Wikipedia: 20, Luc Viatour 22r.

cover stories

the**people**

the**moves**

the**talk**

THE REAL ACTION STARS!

Action stars such as Taylor Lautner and Angelina Jolie are famous for their exciting films, in which they leap from exploding cars, hang from helicopters and abseil down skyscrapers. So, how do they do it? It is all down to the work of stuntmen and stuntwomen. While these tough professionals perform seemingly impossible feats, the A-list stars may be sipping tea in their trailers!

To the extreme

Stuntmen and stuntwomen are highly skilled, world-class athletes. Their job is to do dangerous things in a safe way so that they look amazing on screen. These stunt doubles step in for main characters when things get tough.

Risky business

Stunt sequences are carefully planned to make them as safe as possible. However, stuntmen and stuntwomen have to take risks. They must perform moves over and over, until they look just right on screen. From bruises to broken bones, injuries are all part of a day's work.

Professional hero

It takes years of training and experience to become a stuntperson. After all, stunt teams only want to work with people who can perform feats safely. In return, stunt professionals get to travel to amazing locations, work with stars and see themselves on screen. No two days are the same, so stunts are unlike

Action all-rounders

A stuntperson's job does not end on a film set. They must train hard each day to keep their bodies in excellent condition. They also need to practise different activities. For example, they must be good at combat sports such as martial arts and boxing, gymnastics, trampolining, high-diving, outdoor sports such as swimming, horse riding, motor racing and extreme sports such as free running and rock climbing.

LUCI 'STEEL' ROMBERG

Radar expert Luci Romberg is a champion gymnast, free runner and a leading Hollywood stuntwoman. She tells Radar what it's like to work in film, TV and live shows.

How did you get into stunts?

When I was in college, one of my gymnastics teammates began doing acting and stunts. She convinced me to try it. It wasn't easy. It took years of hard work and dedication. You also need a bit of luck to meet people who will give you jobs.

What is the most dangerous stunt you've performed?

Rolling underneath an articulated lorry that was going at nearly 50 kph!

Do you feel scared when you perform?

Film and TV stunts are well planned and, so far, I have always felt safe because I trust the people around me. If I don't have the skills for a particular job, I'll turn it down and recommend someone else. I am smart about accepting my limits and not taking unnecessary risks.

What films and TV shows have you worked on?

I've performed stunts in more than 40 films and TV shows, such as *Indiana Jones and the Kingdom of the Crystal Skull* (2008) and *Green Lantern* (2011).

What do you do when you're not shooting a film or TV show?

As well as film and TV, many stunt pros work in live shows. I play Peter Pan in a live show at Disneyland. A pirates' ship is my office. What's cooler than that?!

How do you keep fit?

I do free running, hiking, biking, running and boxing.

Have you ever been injured?

I've been really lucky so far. I've only had small injuries such as painful knees, sprained ankles and broken fingers.

What advice do you have for someone wanting to become a stuntperson?

Train hard – you will need to reach a professional standard in several sports to do this job. Never give up, and don't let *anyone* tell you that you can't do something!

Find out more about Luci at www.luciromberg.com

JACKIE CHAN

Superstar stuntman

Jackie performs one of his legendary martial arts stunts in *Around the World in 80 Days*.

Career highlights

1962 landed his first acting role at eight years old in *Seven Little Valiant Fighters*

1979 directed his first movie *Fearless Hyena*

2001 starred in *Rush Hour 2*: one of the most successful martial arts films ever made

2008 voiced a monkey in the hit animation *Kung Fu Panda*

2010 starred in blockbuster *The Karate Kid*

THE STATS

Name: Chan Kong-Sang (Jackie Chan)
Born: 7 April 1954
Place of birth: Hong Kong, China
Personal life: Married with one son
Job: Actor, filmmaker, stunt performer and businessman

Type 'Jackie Chan: my stunts' into www.youtube.com to find out more about Jackie Chan's story.

Kung fu kid

Jackie's passion for martial arts began when he was very young. Every morning, he got up early to practise kung fu with his dad. When Jackie was seven, his parents enrolled him in Hong Kong's China Drama Academy. He spent ten years learning martial arts, acrobatics and acting, but was never taught to read and write.

Stunt star

In his late teens, Jackie began to win stuntman roles in Chinese-language martial arts films. He would try anything. His fearless attitude impressed Hong Kong filmmakers. When he was 21, Jackie landed his first starring role, in *New Fist of Fury*. He was full of creative ideas, and liked to introduce new stunts and comedy into his martial arts films. Jackie became a big star in Asia.

'Superstunt' king

Jackie's ultimate dream was to be a global superstar, which meant making films in Hollywood. His big break came when he made the hit film *Rumble in the Bronx* (1995). Jackie's sensational stunt expertise caught the eye of Hollywood film producers. He soon made many more Hollywood films and became a sought-after A-list star.

Hole in the head

Audiences loved Jackie's carefully choreographed 'superstunts', but they were risky. Jackie was injured many times. He was almost killed when he jumped from a castle wall onto a tree, and fell to the ground. The impact made a hole in his skull, and Jackie underwent immediate surgery. He still has the hole – and a plastic plug to hold in his brains!

Global empire

Jackie has used his fame to help charities and start many businesses, including a stunt school. He still makes films, but now he is so famous that he uses stunt doubles himself! He takes roles in many different types of film, saying, 'I want all the audience to know that not only can I fight, I can really act.'

GLASS FALL

The glass fall is a dramatic stunt in which a stuntperson smashes through a window or glass door, to simulate a fall or jump. This dangerous stunt can result in severe cuts if performed badly, so only the most experienced stuntpeople attempt it.

Essential preparation

- Stunt coordinators ensure windows and doors are fitted with break-away or tempered glass
- Protective clothing
- Bags of nerves!

Why do it?

Scenes in which actors fall or are pushed through glass make exciting viewing. With the use of special glass, these stunts can look extremely convincing. However, crashing through glass is very risky and should be done only by a fully trained stunt professional.

HOW IT'S DONE

1. Two types of glass are used: 'tempered' and 'break-away'. They both break more easily than standard glass upon impact. Tempered glass shatters into sharp pieces, while break-away glass falls to the ground as small blunt pieces, which makes it less dangerous to work with.

2. If working with tempered glass, the stuntperson puts on a protective body suit.

3. A member of the stunt team called an FX person stands ready to activate a device that triggers the break in the glass. The FX person and stuntperson must time the moves perfectly, otherwise the tempered glass will break before the stuntperson falls through it!

4. Break-away glass can be broken by the performer, which makes it easier to use.

LANDING THE PRIZE

Stuntmen and stuntwomen are calling for their work to be recognised with Hollywood's top prize – an Academy Award.

An Oscar category for Best Stunt Coordination was suggested in 1999. Although the Academy rejected it in 2005, campaigners hope it may still be accepted one day.

The ultimate award

The awards, known as Oscars, are handed out every year to the film industry's top people, from actors to make-up artists. Yet despite doing the most dangerous work on a film set, there is still no category for stunt performers.

Hollywood's heroes

The campaign to recognise Hollywood's 'unsung heroes' began over 20 years ago. Famous filmmakers, including Steven Spielberg and Martin Scorsese, have shown their support. Actor and politician Arnold Schwarzenegger said, 'Without them [stuntpeople] there would be no action heroes. In fact, there would be no movies.' Stuntmen and stuntwomen have thrilled fans of the most famous Oscar-winning films, from *Titanic* (1997) to the *Lord of the Rings* trilogy (2001–2003).

Keeping it special

The Academy of Motion Picture Arts and Sciences rarely adds new awards. It is worried that too many categories will make the Oscars less special. However, in 1967, a one-off Oscar was awarded to stuntman Yakima Canutt, for his lifetime of remarkable work. Stunt coordinator Ken Bates also won a special prize in 1993. Several groups now say that there should be an annual award for people that risk their lives on camera.

Red carpet role-call

Despite the calls to provide them with an Academy category, many stunt professionals are happy to stay out of the spotlight. They believe their job is to make the audience think that its favourite actor is the one racing a car or winning a fight. But if other members of the profession are successful in their bid to be recognised at the Oscars, the on-set action heroes may find themselves standing side-by-side on the red carpet with their film-star doubles!

ACTION HERO

My story by Mark Wagner

I grew up doing gymnastics and drama classes. Then I started to perform circus acrobatics with the world famous Cirque du Soleil. I met some stunt pros who all told me my background was perfect for stunt work, so I decided to give it a go.

My big break was in *Spider-Man* (2002). I got to perform major stunts in front of important people in the movie business. The most dangerous was a scene in which Spider-Man dives off a bridge to save Mary Jane and a tram full of children. I had to fall 60 metres towards rocks with a stuntwoman attached to me!

The hardest and most unusual stunt I've ever pulled is a sword fight on top of a huge, rolling wheel in *Pirates of the Caribbean: Dead Man's Chest* (2006). We spent three months working out how to make it happen. We ended up running backwards on a five-metre wheel, while fighting, with only a small wire to catch us if we fell. That scene won me my second Taurus World Stunt Award for Best Fight.

I've been lucky enough to avoid big injuries, but I've had many bumps and bruises. In one fight scene, I was hit in the face by a wooden plank and needed over 30 stitches in and around my mouth!

I love performing wire stunts, and my dream stunt is the decelerator – jumping off a high building with a wire attached. My advice to anyone wanting to follow in my footsteps is to train hard, know your abilities and do your research. It's a long road, but the pay-off is pretty awesome.

FALL OUT!

You're standing on the roof of a ten-storey building. Your heart pounds as you walk towards the edge. The dizzying drop makes your stomach lurch. Your body says run away, but your brain tells you to keep going. You're a tough stunt pro, and you've been hired to jump off the roof in a ball of flames.

And action!

Your eyes lock on the air bag below. From 30 metres up, it looks just as hard as the tarmac. The cast and crew scurry around like an army of ants, making last minute checks on the cameras pointed in your direction. They are relying on you. You begin psyching yourself up for the jump. The assistant tells you to prepare for a blaze that is about to light up your body suit. You've done it before, but every time feels like the first. If it goes wrong, you could really hurt yourself. The second unit director shouts, 'Roof Jump. Take 1. Action!' The slap of the clapboard is your cue to leap.

The rush

Your heart races as you accelerate downwards. You can feel the heat on your back from the fire, while air rushes past your face like a jet stream. All you can see is the ground rushing towards you! Your training kicks in, and you control your body for a safe landing. Bang! You hit the air bag, but the adrenalin rushing through your veins means you barely feel the impact.

It's a wrap

As you roll onto the solid ground, the safety team cover you in a froth of foam. The fire is out, and a round of applause ripples around the set. Everyone's happy with the take, and you know that it will look great on the big screen. The reaction from the cast and crew is the best – you're part of an awesome team. Nothing beats the thrill of a day's work.

PAUL DARNELL

THE STATS

Name: Paul 'Diddy' Darnell
Born: 17 March 1976
Place of birth: Gloucester, Virginia, USA
Home: LA, California, USA
Job: Stunt professional and free running legend

Find out more about Paul Darnell at www.pauldarnell.com

Jumping into stunts

As a teenager, Paul loved watching the creative stunts in Jackie Chan films and soon realised that he wanted to perform stunts for a living. In 2007, he moved to LA and founded his own free running and parkour group, called Tempest. His goal was to 'push the limits of what is physically possible and add some style to it'. Training was fun and an amazing workout, so Paul kept getting better and better. After Tempest performed at the Taurus World Stunt Awards in 2007, Paul began landing stunt jobs in movies.

Passion for life

Paul has become a star himself. In 2011, he performed in the hit film *Water for Elephants* and starred in a new TV show called *Jump City*. He has also opened the Tempest Academy, where people can learn stunt skills. Paul's passion for life is summed up by his own motto: 'Explore your world... set goals and *never* pass on a once-in-a-lifetime opportunity.'

Sporty start

As a child, Paul (above right) loved doing anything physical. He played basketball, baseball and tennis at school. His weekends were filled with everything from breakdancing to BMX-ing. He and his friends even made up a sport called XJ (extreme jumping). When Paul saw a TV show about parkour, he realised that there were people out there doing XJ using proper techniques. He was on a mission to find out more about the extreme sport.

Twilight fever

Paul's amazing moves won him the role of stunt double to one of Hollywood's hottest stars, Robert Pattinson (above left), in the *Twilight* films of 2008 and 2011. He hit the headlines when Robert name-checked him as he collected an MTV Movie Award for Best Fight.

JAW-DROPPING JAPES

Long before filmmakers needed stunt professionals, daredevils performed stunts for excited and shocked crowds. Trapeze artists, sword swallowers and extraordinary horse riders have pulled crowds to circus shows for hundreds of years. History is packed with the thrills and spills of stunt performance.

One of Houdini's most famous stunts was his 'Handcuff Challenge', in which he escaped from chains around his hands, feet and neck.

The Great Houdini

Harry Houdini was one of the first people to turn stunts into entertainment. In the late-1800s, his 'impossible' escapes and endurance tricks made him one of the world's most popular entertainers. In the early-1900s, he appeared in some of the very first silent movies, becoming one of Hollywood's first action heroes.

Death plunge

Thrill seekers around the world followed Houdini's lead and tried to become rich and famous by performing stunts. Many have plunged over North America's most powerful waterfall, the thunderous Niagara Falls. The first to succeed was a 63-year-old woman who dreamed of being famous. Annie Taylor (1838–1921) made the 54-metre drop in a wooden barrel in 1901 – and survived! Several 'stunters' have died attempting to copy her.

Higher, further, faster

Fast-moving motor vehicles gave stuntpeople a new way to wow the crowds. Evel Knievel (1938–2007) became known as 'King of the Daredevils' for leaping his motorbike over cars, buses, trucks and even canyons. Aeroplanes were also used for adrenalin-fuelled stunts. The world-famous Red Arrows Aerobatic team, formed in 1965, carries out daring displays in nine super-fast jets.

Today's action film and TV scenes often feature dangerous manoeuvres, such as jumps from helicopters and planes.

Real-life action hero

Some of the most exhilarating stunts are not done for money or fame, but for the challenge. In 1974, Philipe Petit shocked the world by stringing a steel cable between the towers of New York's World Trade Center, and walking across it without a safety harness! He made the trip – an incredible 400 metres from the ground – eight times. Today, another Frenchman, Alain Robert, makes headlines by free climbing the world's tallest buildings.

Type 'Alain Robert' and 'Philipe Petit' into www.youtube.com to see some of their amazing stunts.

Fantastic film stunts

From the 1960s and 1970s, new technology helped film stunts become bigger, better and more realistic. Air bags allowed stuntpeople to fall from enormous heights. Air rams helped stunt teams to create breathtaking car chases. Today, stunt coordinators and performers continue to perfect techniques and equipment, and every year, more daring and inventive stunts keep audiences glued to the screen.

TRICKS OF THE TRADE

Dramatic car crashes, fearsome fight scenes and extreme explosions electrify the big screen. Stunt teams use technical tricks to capture dangerous-looking action, while ensuring that performers stay as safe as possible.

Look before you leap

Stuntmen and stuntwomen put their lives in the hands of stunt coordinators, who plan and prepare each stunt. Before anyone leaps off a building or drives a car off a bridge, safety measures are put in place based on careful calculations. The next step is to rehearse the stunt meticulously.

Staged fight!

Stage combat alters real fighting moves to make them more exciting to watch. Stunt fighters use a well-rehearsed sequence of moves to create a performance that looks just like an actual fight. All stunt fights are carefully performed so that the stuntpeople are not actually hurt.

Computer wizards

Computer-generated imagery (CGI) or 'special effects', help to make film and TV stunts safer. Life-like explosions, floods, fires and fights can be added as computer graphics. Safety equipment, such as cables and air bags, can be removed from the final pictures.

Stunt coodinators are on hand to make sure that safety equipment is fully functioning before a stunt begins.

However, no stunt is risk-free. Every year, many stuntmen and stuntwomen are injured, and some are killed. Stunt coordinators like to work only with people they trust to train hard and follow instructions. This makes the industry very hard to get into.

Stunt car chases are rehearsed for weeks or even months to ensure that nothing goes wrong during filming.

Stuntpeople rehearse routines made up of punches and kicks that do not actually harm the other person, although they seem to on-screen.

Many of the dramatic effects seen in action films, such as explosions, are CGI magic, which is used to add explosions and flames to a stunt shot after filming.

23

STUNT SPEAK

Use the Radar guide to learn the lingo and sound like a stunt pro.

abseil
to travel down a vertical surface using a rope

air bag
a bag filled with air to cushion high falls and collisions

air ram
a piece of equipment used in stunts to flip vehicles or people into the air

CGI
computer generated imagery, such as fireballs, that are created with software and added to scenes in films

choreograph
to plan a series of moves for the performance of a dance or stunt

free climbing
climbing without using fixed safety ropes

free running
a sport like parkour, with extra acrobatics and creativity

full body burn
when a stuntperson moves through a wall of fire

loop the loop
a trick in which an aircraft or other vehicle does a complete circle

parkour
a sport that involves running, jumping and climbing over obstacles in an urban area

second unit director
the director of stunts and other shots not involving the stars in a film

set
scenery built for a play, TV show or film

stage combat
a harmless fighting technique used by actors to look like real fighting

stunt coordinator
an experienced stuntman or stuntwoman who plans and oversees stunts

stunt double
also called a body double; a stuntman or stuntwoman who stands in for an actor, performing as a particular character in the film

Stuntpeople are trained to carry out dangerous free climbing moves.

stunt sequence

a carefully planned set of moves, tricks or stunts that are filmed in one go

Taurus World Stunt Awards

an award ceremony held each year for stunt professionals

wire

a wire to which a stuntperson is connected to ensure his or her safety

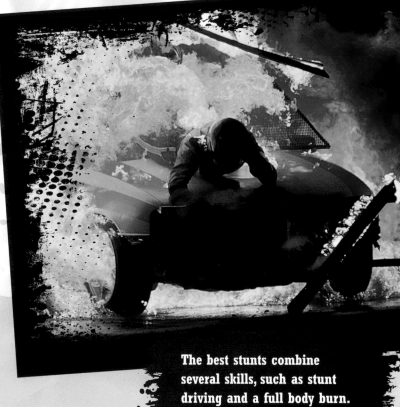

The best stunts combine several skills, such as stunt driving and a full body burn.

GLOSSARY

adrenalin

a hormone found in the human body that causes the heart to beat faster and gives a stuntperson a 'rushing' feeling

articulated lorry

a large lorry with a cab attached to one or more trailers

clapboard

a device used at the start of a film or TV scene. It makes a noise that helps to coordinate the pictures and sound during editing

dedication

commitment to a task

endurance

the ability to get through something difficult without giving up

extinguishes

when someone puts out a fire

kung fu

a Chinese martial art

name-check

to mention someone by name

pro

short for professional; someone who is paid to perform stunts

take

a scene filmed in one go

trailer

where the stars of a film relax and sleep when they are on set

trilogy

a series of three, for instance three films

NO LIMITS

Pro stuntmen and stuntwomen pushed their minds and bodies to the limit to carry out these world-beating stunts.

Must be Maddo

Who: Robbie 'Maddo' Maddison
When: 29 March 2008
Where: Melbourne, Australia
What: Longest ramp jump on a motorcycle
How: Maddo launched his bike 106.98 metres through the air

Jumping Jacquie

Who: Jacquie de Creed
When: 1983
Where: Santa Pod Raceway, UK
What: Long distance Car Ramp Jump
How: Stuntwoman Jacquie became world-famous when she rocketed 70.7 metres through the air in a 1969 Ford Mustang

Champion survivor

Who: Evel Knievel
When: 1938–2007
Where: USA
What: Most bones broken in a lifetime
How: Daredevil Knievel broke 35 different bones in his body during his stunt career

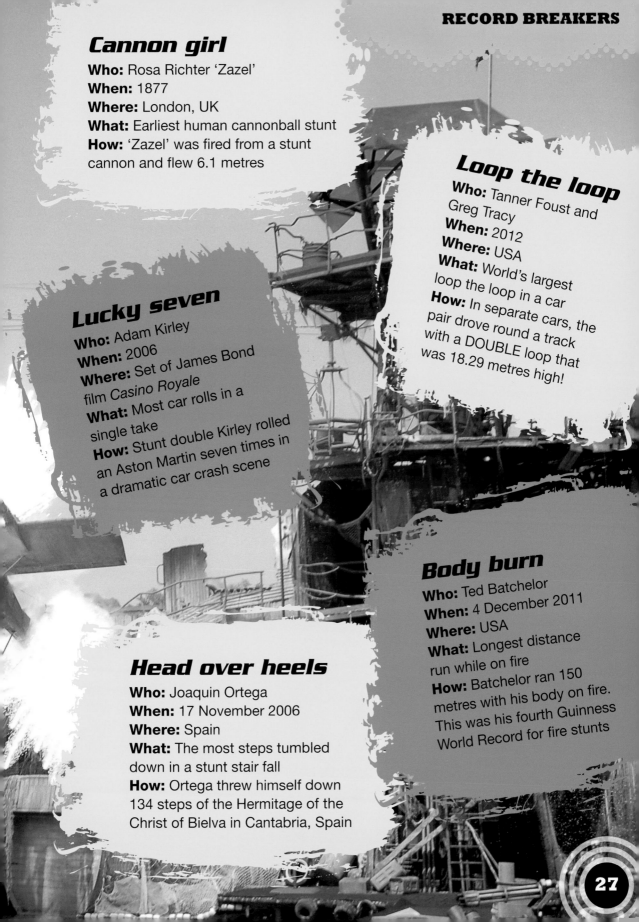

Cannon girl

Who: Rosa Richter 'Zazel'
When: 1877
Where: London, UK
What: Earliest human cannonball stunt
How: 'Zazel' was fired from a stunt cannon and flew 6.1 metres

Loop the loop

Who: Tanner Foust and Greg Tracy
When: 2012
Where: USA
What: World's largest loop the loop in a car
How: In separate cars, the pair drove round a track with a DOUBLE loop that was 18.29 metres high!

Lucky seven

Who: Adam Kirley
When: 2006
Where: Set of James Bond film *Casino Royale*
What: Most car rolls in a single take
How: Stunt double Kirley rolled an Aston Martin seven times in a dramatic car crash scene

Body burn

Who: Ted Batchelor
When: 4 December 2011
Where: USA
What: Longest distance run while on fire
How: Batchelor ran 150 metres with his body on fire. This was his fourth Guinness World Record for fire stunts

Head over heels

Who: Joaquin Ortega
When: 17 November 2006
Where: Spain
What: The most steps tumbled down in a stunt stair fall
How: Ortega threw himself down 134 steps of the Hermitage of the Christ of Bielva in Cantabria, Spain

STUNT STARS

These outstanding stunt professionals have performed some of the most amazing feats ever seen on screen.

1. Joe Canutt

This incredible stuntman could have been killed when he was flipped out of a racing chariot being pulled by four galloping horses in the film *Ben Hur* (1959). Instead, the brave stunt double pulled himself out of the path of the thundering hooves, and back onto the chariot to finish filming the scene! The stunt was directed by Joe's dad, Yakima Canutt, who was world-famous for his death-defying stunts in films such as *Stagecoach* (1939).

2. Simon Crane

During a hijack scene in the film *Cliffhanger* (1993), stuntman Simon Crane performed one of the world's most dangerous and expensive stunts: sliding down a cable between two flying aeroplanes. The film's star, Sylvester Stallone, is reported to have cut his fee by £600,000 (US$1 million) to pay for this amazing scene.

3. Gary Powell

James Bond films are famous for their daring and dangerous stunts. Gary Powell topped previous Bond chase scenes by flipping a speedboat into a 360° spin in *The World Is Not Enough* (1999). If the boat had landed on its roof, his head would have been ripped off. The 15-minute chase took a total of seven weeks to shoot on the River Thames in London, UK.

4. Michelle Yeoh

This incredible stuntwoman is one of a few actresses who performs her own stunts. In *Supercop* (1992), she pulled off one of the most dangerous stunts ever done by a woman: jumping a dirt bike onto the roof of a moving train. She was then cast as a Bond girl in *Tomorrow Never Dies* (1997) and became a Hollywood star. Michelle went on to wow audiences in the film *Crouching Tiger, Hidden Dragon* (2000), in which she performed dazzling fight scenes and stunts.

Type 'Ziyi Zhang vs. Michelle Yeoh' into www.youtube.com to see one of Michelle's amazing fight stunts in *Crouching Tiger, Hidden Dragon*.

5. Wayne Michaels

The amazing bungee jump off a 229-metre-high dam performed by Wayne Michaels in *GoldenEye* (1995) is one of the most famous James Bond stunts. The bungee cord had to be exactly the right length: too long and he would hit the ground, too short, and he would risk bouncing against the lethal steel rods that covered the dam wall. As he hurtled towards the ground, Wayne calmly acted the part of Bond reaching for a gun.

FIREBALL

Stunts involving fire can add breathtaking drama to a film. However, they are extremely dangerous and are performed only by a highly experienced team.

Essential preparation

- Full safety checks
- Fire and ambulance crew on stand-by
- Precision timing

Why do it?

Stuntpeople can add an authenticity to a fire scene that cannot be created by a computer. However, the stunt is a high-risk procedure that requires hours of careful planning and strenuous safety checks to ensure that nothing goes wrong.

How it's done

1. The stuntperson puts on several layers of fire-resistant clothing, including a special protective hood and gloves.

2. The stunt coordinating team checks that the protective clothing fully covers the stuntperson so that no flesh will be exposed to the flames.

3. The stunt coordinating team then coats the stuntperson in a flammable gel.

4. The team signals to the camera crew and director that they are ready to begin the stunt and to start filming.

5. The flammable gel is lit, and the action sequence is filmed. Throughout, the stuntperson wears a face mask through which they can safely breathe.

6. The stunt coordinating team extinguishes the flames and checks that the stuntperson is unharmed.

ACTION LIST

People to talk to

Would you like to leap into the amazing world of stunts? Start by getting good at action-packed sports, from martial arts and gymnastics to horse riding. Be prepared to work hard – couch potatoes need not apply!

The British Action Academy

Check out the skills you need to be accepted on to the British JISC Stunt Register. The British Action Academy will even hold a Movie Action Workshop for 7- to 11-year-olds at your school: **www.britishactionacademy.com**

Free running

Free running and parkour are a great way into stunts, and can be done by anyone, anywhere! Before you start, contact an organisation that teaches parkour skills to beginners, such as:
www.parkourgenerations.com
www.norwich-parkour.co.uk

Check out the stuntmen and stuntwomen's Association of Motion Pictures at:
www.stuntmen.com
www.stuntwomen.com

Reads & Apps

Mission Impossible: Stunt Crews – Death-defying Feats by Jim Pipe (Wayland, 2011)

Download *Top Gear: Stunt School* – the BBC's stunt driving app that lets you try out crazy stunts. Find it at:
www.itunes.com
https://market.android.com

INDEX